Enjoy your Stimula...

Whitney Caskins

For Wesleigh

Math ABC's

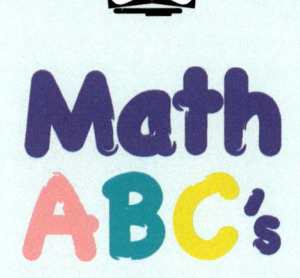

by Dr. Whitney B. Gaskins

Illustrated by Halie Jo Bryer

Wesleigh and Waylen's STEMulating Adventures

Hi, I'm Wesleigh!

and I'm Waylen!

Come on won't you learn with me?
It's time to do Math ABC's!

Aa

Addition

Wesleigh has two widgets,
Waylen has four, put them together,
they have fun with more.

Bb

Bracket

Shows the first step when beginning to solve. Things in between are what is involved

$2x$

Cc

Coefficient

The number in front lets us know just how much we should grow.

$$\frac{1}{2} = \qquad \frac{1}{3} =$$

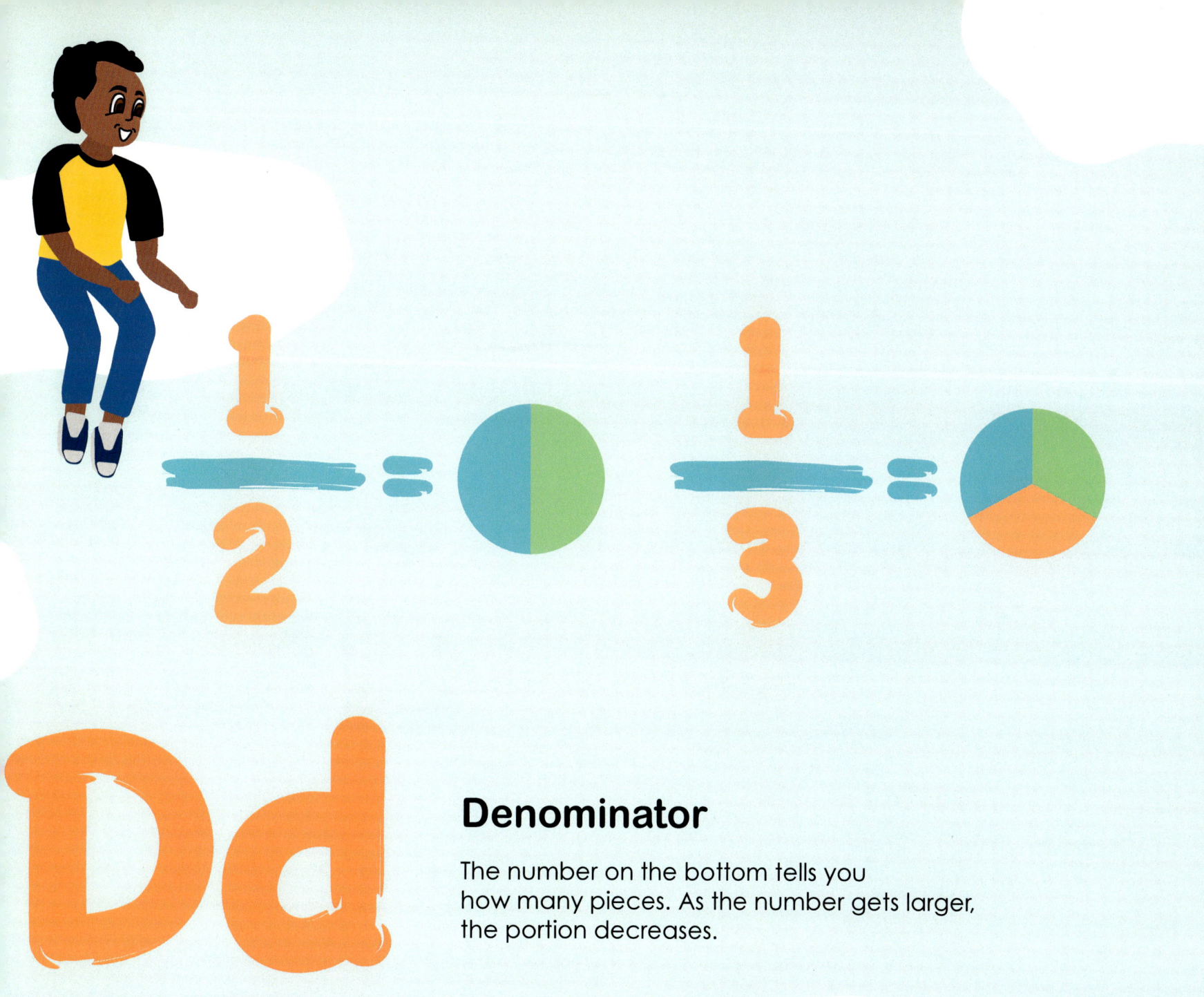

Dd

Denominator

The number on the bottom tells you how many pieces. As the number gets larger, the portion decreases.

$$E=mc^2$$

Ee

Equation

Math's version of a sentence that contains an equal sign. When the left equals the right, both sides feel fine.

Ff

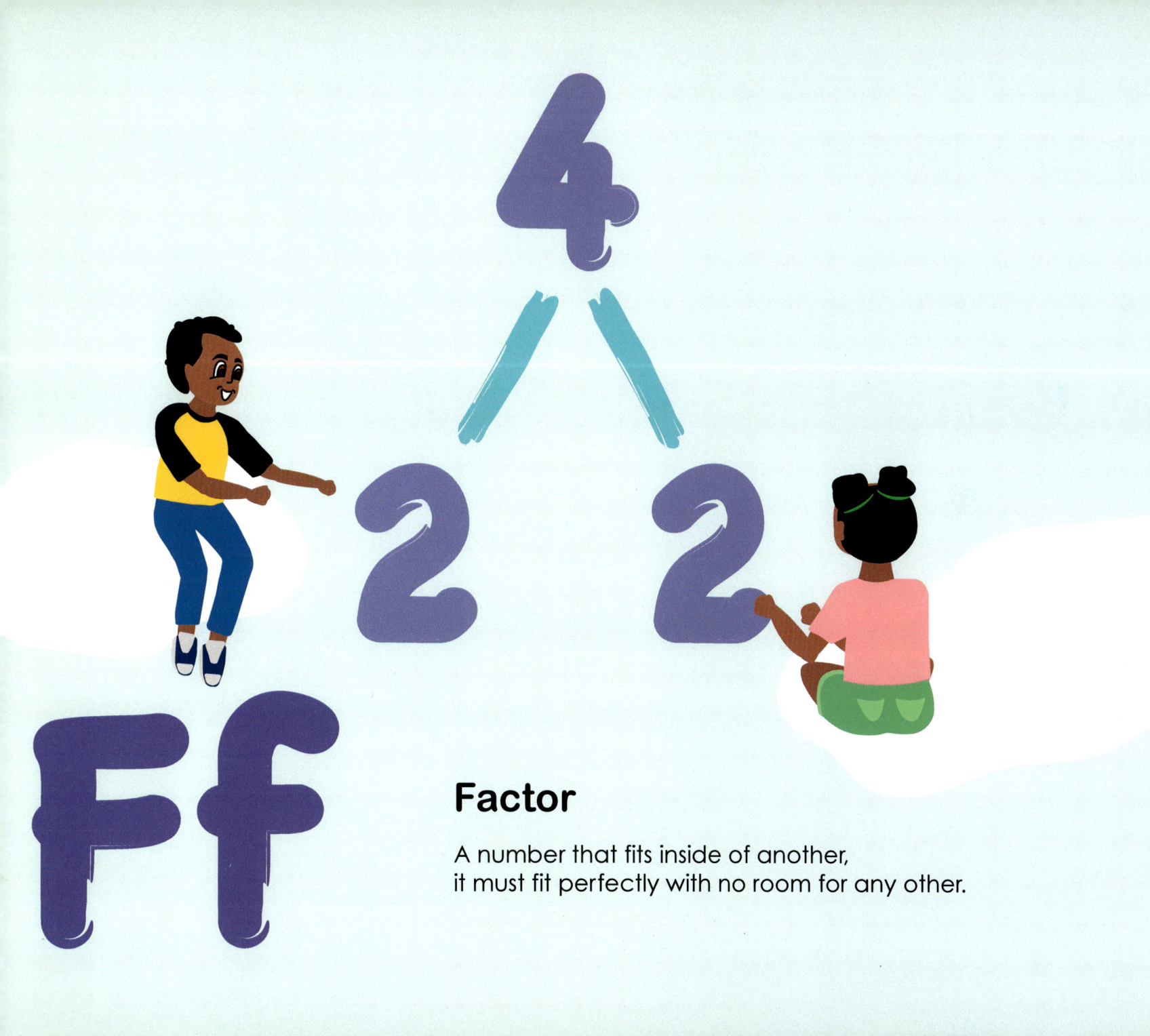

Factor

A number that fits inside of another,
it must fit perfectly with no room for any other.

$y=x^2$

$y=x^3$

Gg

Graph

A graph is a picture that shows great information.
When the numbers change, it's a new creation.

Hh

Horizontal

When the direction goes from left to right,
you create a line with no end in sight.

Ii

Integer

Integers are numbers that span the entire line.
Positive, negative, and even zero are fine.

steps

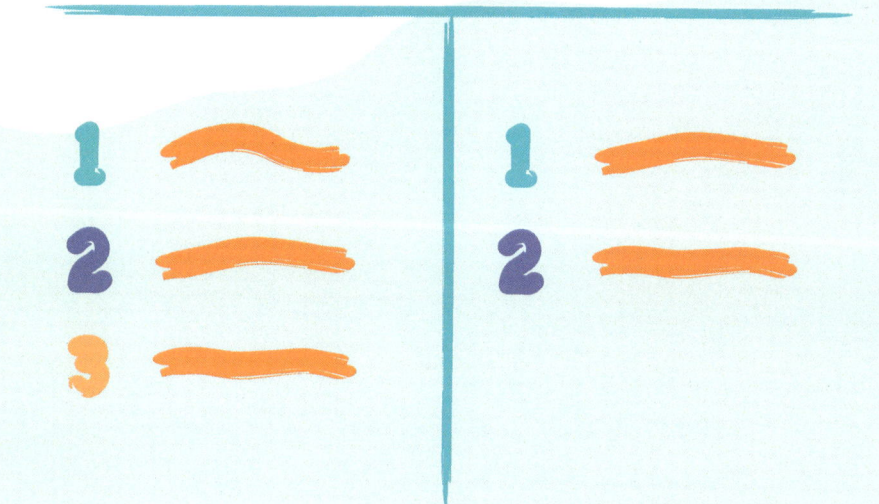

1 ___
2 ___
3 ___

1 ___
2 ___

Jj

Justification

List out your steps and see what you've done. Make sure to list them one by one.

Kk

Kilo

It adds three zeroes to make numbers larger.
It can also make trips seem so much farther.

Long Division

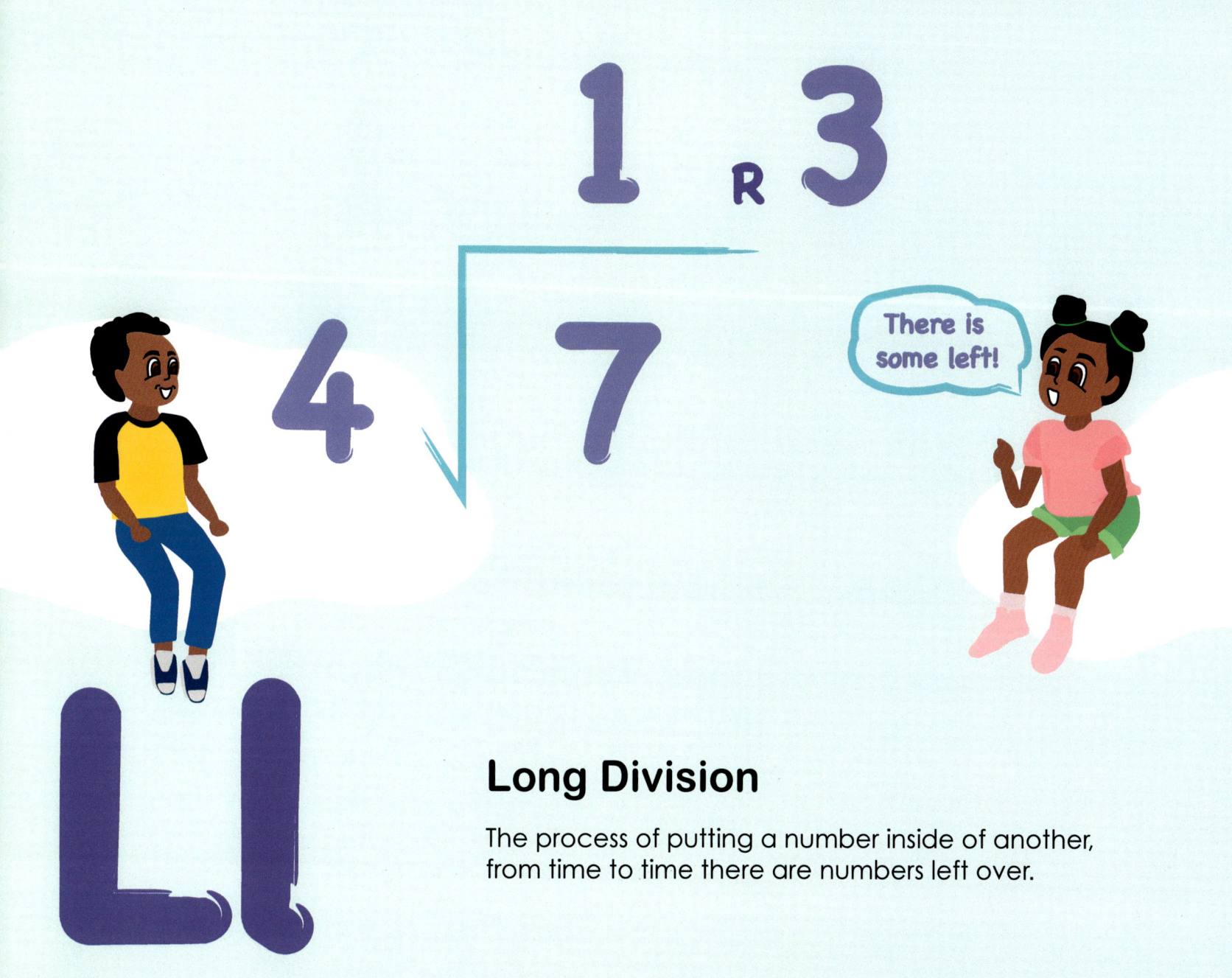

The process of putting a number inside of another, from time to time there are numbers left over.

$2 \times 3 = 6$

$2 + 2 + 2 = 6$

Multiplication

The number of times something is added to itself.
It's called fast addition, if nothing else.

$\frac{1}{3}$ $\frac{2}{3}$

I want 1!

I want 2!

Nn

Numerator

The numerator is the number on top of any fraction, it tells you how many parts you're interested in havin'.

1. $()$ Parentheses

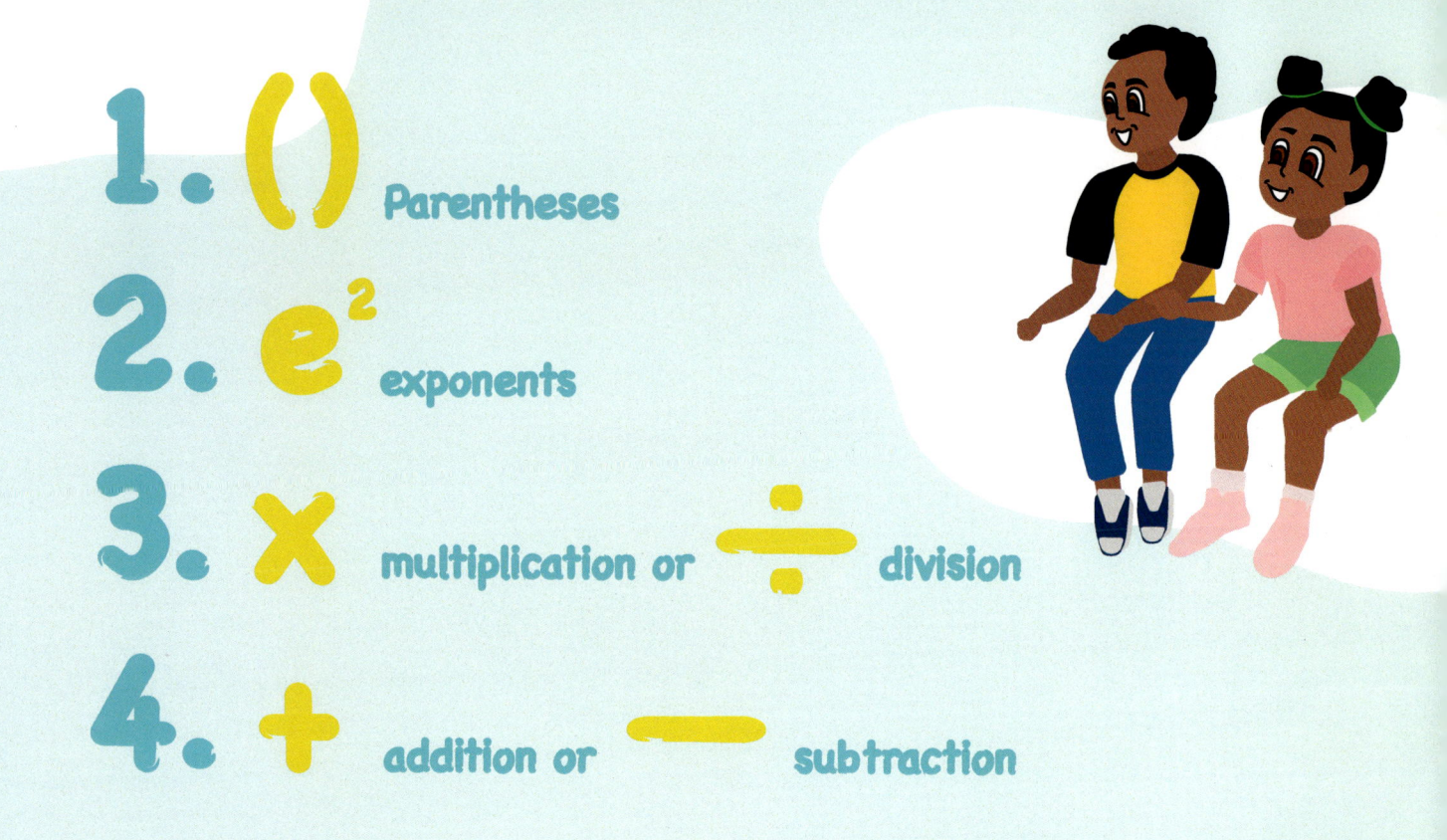

2. e^2 exponents

3. $\times$ multiplication or $\div$ division

4. $+$ addition or $-$ subtraction

Oo

Order of Operations

Known by most as PEMDAS, it tells you the directions to follow so you don't get lost.

Pp

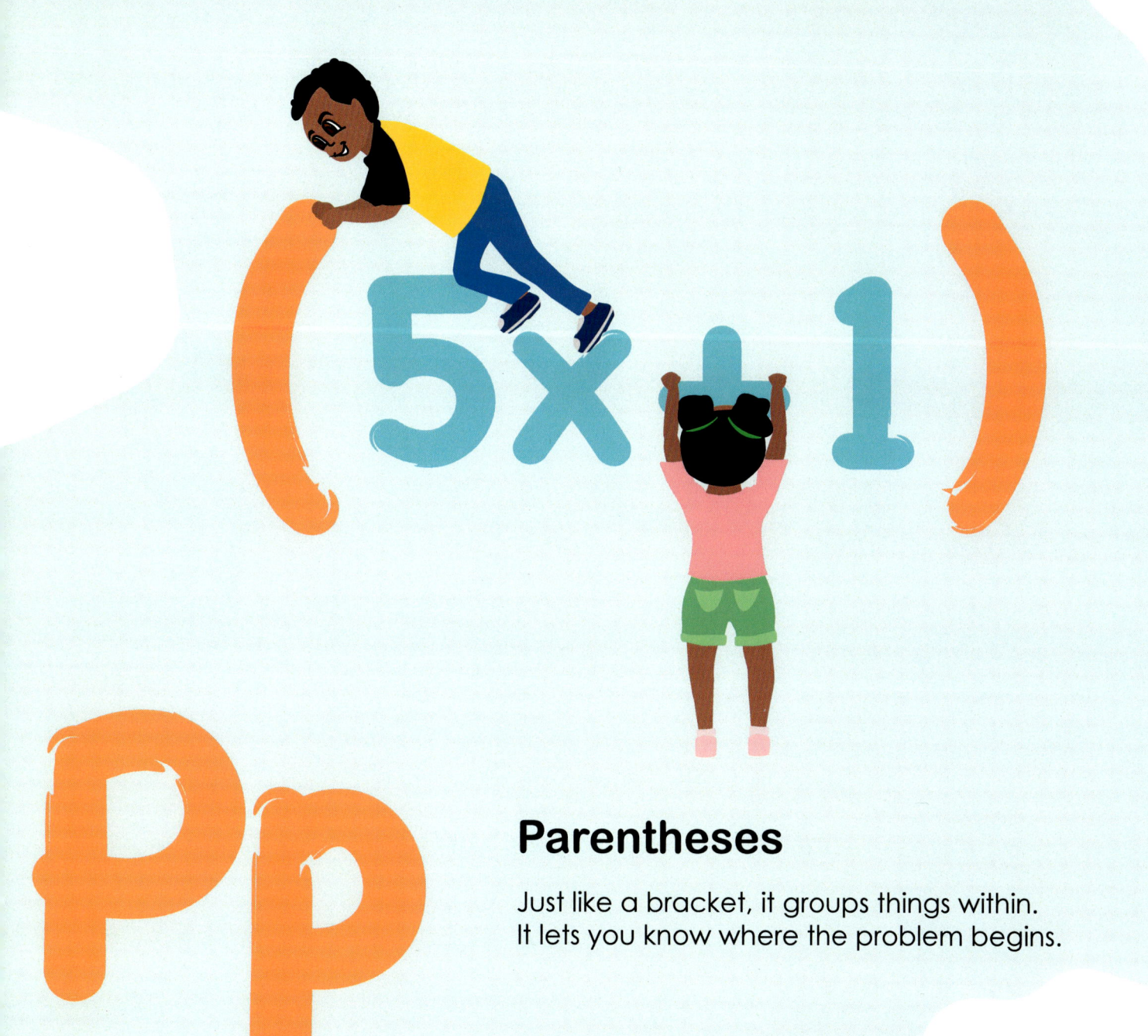

Parentheses

Just like a bracket, it groups things within.
It lets you know where the problem begins.

Qq

Quotient

The number you get after you divide,
it's the number on top,
not on the in- or outside.

Rr

Remainder

The number that is left over after you divide.
It gives you an answer that is precise or just right.

$$5-3=2$$

Ss

Subtraction

When you take away a number from one with more, you will end up with less than you had before.

Tt

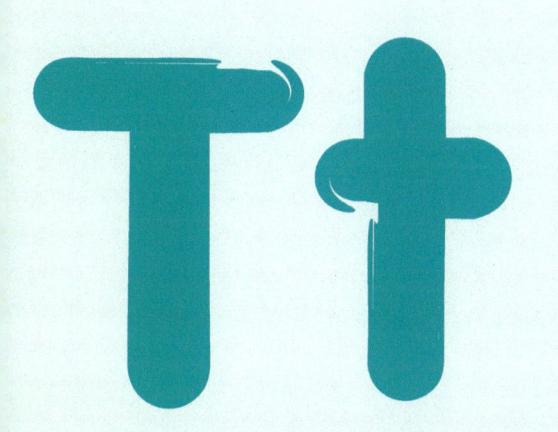

Tally

The marks you make to keep track or score,
cross diagonally every five and keep going for more.

Uu

Unit

It can mean a measure of one and can count inches, feet, yards, or hours of fun.

$$2x + 1 = 5$$
$$x = 2$$

Vv

Variable

An unknown value represented by a letter, when you find what it is you feel so much better.

Ww

Whole Number

Numbers you count from zero to infinity, but if you're looking for negatives, you won't find any.

X-Coordinate

It's a horizontal line that you see on a graph, the values on the right are the positive half.

Y-Coordinate

Numbers are listed up and down on this line, also referred to as the vertical line.

Zz

Z-Coordinate

We use this third line when your graph is 3D.
It's how they make movies come through the TV.

Katherine Johnson

Katherine Johnson was an American mathematician whose calculations of orbital mechanics as a NASA employee were critical to the success of the first and subsequent U.S. crewed spaceflights. During her 35-year career at NASA she earned a reputation for mastering complex manual calculations and helped pioneer the use of computers to perform the tasks. The space agency noted her "historical role as one of the first African-American women to work as a NASA scientist." She is featured in the movie Hidden Figures.

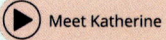

Meet Katherine

Benjamin Banneker

Benjamin Banneker was a free African-American almanac author, surveyor, landowner and farmer who had knowledge of mathematics and natural history. Born in Baltimore County, Maryland, to a free African-American woman and a former slave, Banneker had little or no formal education and was largely self-taught. He became known for assisting Major Andrew Ellicott in a survey that established the original borders of the District of Columbia, the federal capital district of the United States. He is also recognized as the inventor of the clock.

Meet Benjamin

Meet Whitney

Dr. Whitney B. Gaskins is currently an Assistant Dean and Assistant Professor in the University of Cincinnati College of Engineering and Applied Science. She holds a PhD in Biomedical Engineering with a focus on Engineering Education. She has been widely recognized for her work in supporting K-PhD students.

She is the founder of The Gaskins Foundation, which creates pathways for K-12 students to enter into STEM fields by providing free and low cost informal educational opportunities. More information on the foundation can be found at www.thegaskinsfoundation.org.

Dr. Gaskins is also the Principle Investigator of the Removing Obstacles for STEM Education (R.O.S.E.) Lab in Cincinnati, OH. The lab helps create research-based solutions to remove barriers that often prevent members of marginalized groups from entering the STEM workplace.

She currently resides in Cincinnati, OH with her husband, Delano White and son Waylen Delano White.

To Learn More

Meet Whitney

Copyright © 2021 by Dr. Whitney B. Gaskins. Printed in the United States of America.

No part of this publication may be reproduced, distributed, or transmitted in any form or by any means, including photocopying, recording, or other electronic or mechanical methods, without the prior written permission of the publisher, except in the case of brief quotations embodied in critical reviews and certain other noncommercial uses permitted by copyright law. For permission requests, contact Otherside Press.

978-0-9791026-3-9

Attention organizations and schools. Take 33% off and use your book as fundraisers, premiums or gifts. Please contact the publisher:

Otherside Press
P.O. Box 741
Cincinnati, OH 45201
(313) 477-4148

www.othersidepresspub.com
www.whitneygaskins.com